COPING WITH BULLIES

A Gentle Approach

Carolyn Franklin, M.A.

voicedynamicscf@yahoo.com

ISBN: 9781097451388
Imprint: Independently published

Contents

When you're born into this world you come in with pretty much - nothing. You're an adorable baby that eats and sleeps - that's it. You eat and sleep. If you're cold, you yell and someone gets you warm. If you're hungry, you yell, and someone gets you a nice, warm meal. If you're wet, you yell and someone gets you dry. In between cold, hungry and wet, you sleep.

Life is a breeze. No problems.

For the first year, things go pretty much as they should - you yell and get what you want. Hey, this is easy!

Then, things seem to go haywire. You're crawling on the floor on the soft, oriental rug, when, **OW!** Something hit you on the head!

You stop, mid-crawl and yell! No, not just YELL! You sit there, furious and open that big mouth with the two teeth and CRY and YELL! Tears gush out of your mouth and your little body is rigid with anger and pain!

You bumped your head on the piano leg. A piano leg is made of something hard, not soft like Mommie - really hard - and it hurts!

Mommie picks you up and makes the hurt get better.

Later, you're somewhere and lots of other children are there, too. It's a big room with space, big windows, and toys. You see a big, red ball rolling on the floor. You want it, you get it, you're playing with it when - suddenly! Some other person wants the ball and takes it away!

What!

You're indignant! You had that ball! You were playing with that ball! and someone took it away from you - and the big people don't seem to care!

Where's Mommie!!

You've been abandoned!

That was your first experience at being bullied. Someone took the red ball and no Mommy came to help you.

How do you react?

Do you sit and cry?

Do you sit, stunned, wondering what happened?

Do you go after the ball to get it back?

Do you expect a big person to get the ball back for you?

Do you give up and look for something else to play with?

By the time you're two years old, you're pretty much who you're going to be.

NURTURE? NATURE?

Some children are born with aggressive tendencies, some are born quiet, receptive, slow to anger.

Some children have a great deal of energy, of curiosity. They can't sit still; they're constantly pulling at something to see what it is, take it apart; they examine those parts and focus intently on how they work.

One of my friends has two sons, one is 5, a really sweet child. The other is 2 years of energy, determination, focus and the strength of a pit bull.

We tried to visit, impossible. The 2 year old was, literally, tearing my house apart. He tore down my outdoor thermometer from the wall, broke it open to see how it worked. He tried to climb over the deck railing to look at the patio below. He opened the cupboard doors to see what was inside, took everything out, scattered what he could handily reach...

His mother did not sit down to the tea and lunch I had for us, she ran after him every moment to stop some demolition.

I told her to get him into Montessori as soon as possible. My sense of him is that he is a pent-up genius and needs guidance. He is NOT a bully.

Other children are passive, not curious at all about the world with all of its distractions, noise and confusion. They're quiet, easy to manage, happy to be where they are and they don't bother the other children around them.

Much of the time in a child's life, others keep trying to make that child something he's not. Adults assume, "He should not do that! She should do this!..." Should! Shouldn't! Do this! Don't do that!

Constant should's and shouldn't's circle around the child, commands that are confusing and seem to cancel each other out.

SHOULD - OR SHOULDN'T?

So much of the time the "should's" and "shouldn't's" cancel each other out. The thing you did ten minutes ago is suddenly wrong! What happened?

3

Someone gave you a big crayon to color the pictures on the pages in the big book. But the pages were too small, so you went over to the big, white wall where there was plenty of space to make big pictures.

Well, if they didn't want you to color in that big space - the white wall, well, why didn't they say so!

Then you get in trouble because you didn't know something that no one told you!

Life is so confusing! People often say when a baby is born, you don't know how to raise it - it didn't come with a Book of Instructions." Well, neither did Life.

Every day is a blank page. Everyday is a classroom, a learning experience where we have no idea what to learn or not learn.

It's hit or miss.

BULLYING 101

It's bully, bully, bully - from day one! You're forever being told, "Do this! Don't do that! Stop! Start! Sit! Stand! Come here! Go there!…"

Sometimes we term bullying "teaching;" sometimes it's called "guidance". Sometimes it's called "Helping you, it's for your best interests…"

Sometimes what we're told to do is understandable and useful. Other times, it's grating, irritating and annoying.

But, usually we understand the "orders", "instructions" have some reasonable basis and we accept the guidance as for the best.

So, when do "instructions" or "guidance" become "bullying"?

We need "education". Sometimes it's words, sometimes physical, sometimes a demonstration, sometimes miming, hand signals - it depends on the child.

SOCIAL TRAINING, EXPECTATIONS

Every home, every community, every family, has a different idea of how to conduct its life. This idea becomes "Truth" - the way life should be. Habitats of the one family or society believe the way they do things is the right way, the best way, and the only way. Their way is Truth.

Quaker, Amish:

At times, then, a response to bullying may be viewed from different angles. A Quaker or Amish would espouse peace, mental peace and no physical response to the offender, just pray for the offender. This does not necessarily discourage the offender, but it allows the Quaker, Amish to perceive himself as superior, above mortal distress.

Christian:

Usually a Christian will advise, "Turn the other cheek," "Pray for your enemies," "Put on the whole armor of God" and hope that God is listening and will smite the bully. Probably won't happen.

Actually, that's not God's job. That's your job.

God gave us free will and intelligence. We're expected to use these gifts appropriately. Christians expect God to jump in the fray and save their necks. That way, the Christian thinks, "If I'm real good, God will fix it - **I** don't have to get involved!"

Wrong answer.

God helps those who help themselves - and, yes, he does *help*. But you have to put your nose to the wheel.

New Age:

It's a philosophy espousing, "Peace, man, peace," and then you drop out of this world into some plane where bullies dissolve in a purple cloud - man. That thought actually works - but no others do - there are no other thoughts.

> **Karma**: There is no doubt that some day, some where, somehow, retribution will out, revenge will happen for people who wrong you. They'll have to pay and pay hard. Not your concern and not your problem. Your job is to show yourself your inner strength and teach others to leave people alone - mostly, leave you alone.

That takes a lot of inner strength that materializes when you're about 62.

Old Country

People come to America to live - physically, but mentally they're still in the Old Country. They do things the way they have always done, or at least try to. Boys, men, are perceived, usually, as all powerful, and girls are to breed and keep the butter churned.

Dealing with bullying is not an issue. The girl brought it on herself and boys are boys. That old formula has worked for hundreds of years.

It's a little hard on the girls.

Your cultural image

So, think carefully about your culture, your environment, your back-up support before you face down a bully. Does your training, your background, your society allow for you to stand up for yourself? Will you have guilt feelings later or will you feel good about yourself?

Are you really a "peace-nik" because you're scare stiff to face down a bully? If you say you're a peace-full person, do you think that will get you off the hook - away from danger?

CULTURAL MENTAL SUFFERING, CONFUSION, FEAR

There is no stress as insidious, as destructive, as draining, as mental stress - worry. Studying for exams, or immersed in future plans is stressful, dental appointment, yes, stressful, but not destructive.

The worry, the stress, the fear of safety to one's self, to the family, your security, your basic health or financial security can be mentally destructive. It can leave scars that last a lifetime.

> *One of my friends, an adult, is terrified of getting lost. She is so afraid of being lost when she steps out of her home that she only goes to certain places where the path is well known. I have been the driver to functions with her sitting next to me and when she's in an area which is new to her, she panics.*

> *She jumps up and down on the car seat, looks frantically out all the car windows, yells, sobbing - "I don't know where I am! **I don't know where I am!!**..."*

> *I reply, "Well, I do - I know where I am. And I'm driving, so relax!"*

She'll calm down for a minute and then, off to the races!
All over again she panics!

This stems from her childhood. Her mother didn't want her, so "Susie" would be put in the basement under a big box and told to stay there or the spiders would eat her. Susie would sit under that box, alone, for hours peeking through a crack at the sunlight from the cellar windows.

When she got in a car, a "box" and looked out the windows she was "lost" forgotten, the same as in the cellar. She doesn't "know" what's going on outside the "box". It will never be fixed.

Cultural mental suffering for boys

Boys, too much of the time - in fact any amount of time, are verbally compared to a brother, or a successful cousin... Boys are measured by "success" - "you don't measure up - look at Ben, he's successful! What's wrong with you? Act like a man - you'll never amount to much as this rate."

Then on Ben's way to school, some big guy takes his lunch money. Ben's told, "You should'a stood up for yourself! Look'im in the eye! Don't let anyone push you around!"

The guy was really big and ugly.

Cultural mental suffering for girls

Religion is a common base for girls to be bullied. Above all other considerations, starting with Eve, girls are held to higher standards of how we behave. The standards are personal, "Stand up straight. Fix your hair, you're going to wear THAT?" We're chided, scolded and constrained - sit like a lady! - so we will be socially acceptable, groomed for marriage. We're socially held to a higher standard, usually, than boys are.

8

We're bullied before we get off the ground, right at birth, our social and behavioral expectations are pre-planned. Our life is preordained. It may not be said in words, but our behavioral limitations are strongly felt by innuendo as we mature.

Sex abuse is common among young girls, generally by a family member. She is threatened with dire consequences if she tells, disruption of family, a threat to kill her pet. Often girls will cling to a pet for love and acceptance because she has no one else to turn to. Her family is a danger, no one believes her when she tell them what's happening.

The fact that no one listens, no one cares, is the real abuse.

In a great many families, the sons take precedent over the girls. It is believed boys are more important. This is insidious mental suffering - so egregiously unfair - and erroneous.

> *In one of my classes during a speech, a girl commented that she had received a scholarship for excellence in her studies. She had planned on going to a specific school to continue her scholastic advancement when her parents took the scholarship away from her and gave it to her brother. He wanted to play football - chase a ball around a field on his sister's future hopes.*

This treatment is reprehensible. As well as an insult to the daughter, think of the message it sends to the son. Do you think he will have a happy marriage, a happy life, thinking he'll get everything he wants?

We live under strong family social criticism and then we're bullied also by various others; we can get to a breaking point fast. And, when we break, we're told we, "take things too seriously," "get over ourself," "just ignore it, move on, pretend like it didn't happen, you misunderstood their motives, meaning, ideas…"

9

CULTURAL PHYSICAL SUFFERING, PAIN, FEAR

Cultural stress can be very oppressive, smothering at times. You want please your family and please your friends. But some of their expectations are very difficult to reach, and some of the expectations do not interest you at all.

> *One young man I know was an artist. He drew beautiful homes. He wanted to be an architect. His dad took his art supplies, threw them out and said, "You will be a doctor!"*

The boy's spirit was crushed. I don't know if he ever did become a doctor, but if his heart's not in it, neither he nor his patients will do well.

Girls are usually expected to marry and get married in the same tradition as the older community did and also marry a man the community approves of. Sometimes the right man is hard to find so the girls are expected to "settle for what they can get."

Her feelings are not accepted nor important.

Cultural physical suffering for boys

In some cultures it's believed that physical punishment makes a boy into a man.

When a boy gets pushed around, hit, teased, ganged up on, supposedly it's a rite of passage, something boys are supposed to experience and grow from.

Today, in this society, this treatment and attitude are not acceptable. Under these conditions a boy has the right to seek legal help, call the police notify authorities. There is a counselor at most schools where he can get help, guidance and support.

Reporting abuse is difficult when the abuse is at home. The parents simply deny it. The boy may have bruises and scars that would be evidence, but exactly how those bruises and scars got there can be explained away sometimes.

Cultural physical suffering for girls

Another friend of mine, "Rose", was from an ethnic family where the girls were held to tight schedules and controlled ways of thinking. Rosie was particularly bright, but nervous. When her school work wasn't right, or she was made to stand, facing a wall for 2 hours as punishment.

Twice she tried college, but when faced with a test, she froze, shut down, afraid if she made a mistake, she'd have to stand facing the wall for 2 hours. She never graduated from college. Today she's a bitter, hate-filled woman who only relates to her pet dog.

Often, during winter months where there is snow, she was forced to sleep on the front porch. Her mother was a brow-beaten women who never interfered with the husband's decisions. Rosies' brother was treated quite well as a family member in good standing. As of this day, both brother and sister have no contact with each other.

BULLYING IS A TYPE OF "LOVE"

Yes, a "twisted" kind of love.

11

When you love someone, you think about them most of the time. You go to sleep with their name on your lips. You can't concentrate on your studies or projects – all you think about is them. Where ever they are you watch for them, your eyes follow them as they talk to someone else. You wonder what they're doing or saying at that minute.

You can't eat or sleep for dreaming about them.

Bullies do the same thing when they torment you. Their behavior is negative, destructive, but, most of the time they think about you, what you're doing, where you are – all about you.

It is *sick behavior* – these people are disturbed, live an empty life. Instead of being angry with them, feel sorry for them. They may be so jealous of you, your family, good looks – who knows.

They are not mentally healthy. Try not to think about them and waste your good energy to make your life a better place.

But....until then, here are many ideas and strategies to help you cope with the stress.

You must try to get to a mental place where your family and friends can stop helping you - yes! Stop "helping"!! How can *you* stand on your own two feet if others keep trying to prop you up? Very likely the bully will strike at times and places where you're on your own and you have to handle the situation by yourself - very scary sometimes!

You have to get to the point where you can anticipate and steel yourself, to some degree, on how to ignore the bully or put him (her) in their place.

All bully situations are unique; even though the strategies are the same, the specific instances are one-of-a-kind, somewhat out of your control. It's difficult to always be prepared, but one response to bullies most of the time is - *none.*

If at possible, don't respond to their taunts, to their words or behavior - not an easy thing to do. Don't feed the bully your energy, your mind, your "love".

TWO BASIC IDEAS TO UNDERSTAND THE POWER OF BULLIES

1. Who is the bully?

Who am I up against? If you could walk through the head of a bully you might find yourself walking in Fear up to your ankles. A bully night be afraid of Life, scared of being hurt, fear of the unknown, of being alone, powerless and low self-esteem.

The bully may be someone who is abandoned in his (her) family. There's too many people in the home, no one gets the attention, love, support he needs, so that child will create a world where he gets the love he craves. Bullying is a strategy to force others to pay attention to him or her, to feel his strength and "brilliance"

He or she strikes out at the world as a kind of "hurt them before they hurt me" mentality. When someone feels cornered, sees himself as having little value, living in darkness, they may be defensive, aggressive - they have nothing to lose and, perhaps, some thing to gain.

You may have noticed, a bully is rarely alone, usually he or she runs in a gang. When someone needs a companion at all times, he needs protection – he can't tolerate isolation - he's scared of the dark.

The average person can't stop a bully easily, or change his behavior – it's difficult to cope with fear and keep our own balance. The basic goal of the bully is to *get attention* – anyhow, anyway!

2. Who are you?

How much pressure can you tolerate?

Do you break apart easily?

Do you hold everything inside and explode later?

Do you hide, shut down inside when you're hurt?

Do you complain to everyone about what "they" are doing to you?

Do you expect others to step in and stop the problem?

Are you a fighter?

Do you cry when your feelings are hurt?

Do you hate yourself – or them, if someone says something about you?

Do you believe everything they say: They're popular, you're not - they have friends, you don't; they're good in sports, you're not; you're stupid.

Do you feel helpless, alone, no one understands?

There's no one to talk to – you're terrified, scared stiff.

Do you cry easily; are you afraid to be alone – you need friends?

Are you willing to follow whatever your friends do to be "popular"?

Do you loan your "friends" money? Pay for their food? Are you buying them?

WHAT ARE YOU DOING TO ENCOURAGE THE BULLY?

As it says in the Bible, "Know thyself." Never mind what people tell you to do, go by your inner feelings - the *only* person you can *change is yourself. You have no power over a bully.*

You're probably not doing anything deliberately. You're probably doing what you always do. But, why is this going on? Ask a close friend if they have an idea. See what other people are doing who are not bullied. Keep aware of the world around you.

SUPERSTITION

Oddly enough I have found that bullies are very superstitious people. The least little oddball event or thought that is "spooky" or "out of this world," sends them into a panic.

I don't advocate the use of "out-of-this-world" strategies to scare the bully as something like that could backfire in your own life. But it's something to be aware of.

> *There was a woman at my church who played a really dirty trick on me.*
>
> *I got "even" with her by staring at her with "evil" eyes. Every time, she burst in tears. I was amused - I was actually just looking, no evil intended.*
>
> *Her conscience did the rest.*

15

STOCKHOLM SYNDROME

This is a condition where the victim, or target, is so afraid of the bully, he, or she will do whatever it takes to keep the bully happy, sacrifice a friend, if necessary, to save her "protector". If she obeys the abuser, her life is safe. She'll try to be just like the bully so he'll be happy and not hurt her. People who run with bullies may fall into this category – their fear makes them dangerous, treacherous and pathetic.

They have been so mistreated in their own life, they cannot be trusted with your life.

A bully who follows his leader and does exactly what he's told, is a dangerous person.

STANFORD STUDENTS

The YMCA had invited me to talk to 50 college students on "How to Handle Bullies" – that was the title of my presentation. At the time I didn't realize the title had a two-way meaning – how to make bullies behave, or, how to make bullies happy.

My goal is to have bullies behave and leave the "victim" alone. No one wants to be bullied!

These were Stanford students and they not only disagreed with my ideas, they booed me, stamped their feet on the floor and yelled cat-calls! They refused to let me talk - I was appalled and disgusted! They were bullying me! And, they were completely aware of how rude they were!

They sat there, smug, smiling, very pleased that they had shut down my free speech!

I was disgusted.

The woman in charge of the YMCA had no idea how to handle "bullies"; she sat and squirmed throughout the farce. She had that "simpering" smile on her face so typical of people who are emotionally weak.

So, I left, amidst her profound apologies.

The sad part is how both sides missed out. If the Stanford students had any courtesy at all, I would give my side, then listen to their side and we might have both learned something useful from a dialogue. They, no doubt, had some valuable information I could have used to help future "victims".

We'll never know! The point is that if the "elite" of our country cannot take the time to understand and help "victims" - "targets" then we'll have an uphill struggle to help the weaker underdogs of society. Will we face more suicides of victims because of this blatant ignorance?

I am sooooo ashamed for Stanford to put out ambassadors like that.

SOCIAL MEDIA

Social media has no face, no conscience, no interface; it can be an insidious weapon to destroy people. Today this is possibly the most dangerous bully created. It's a perfect tool to hurt people, lie about them, make fun of them and manipulate them, and not be held accountable.

Don't be dragged into this craziness – *turn the media off*. People who rely on Social media for human interaction do so because they don't have enough intelligence to relate to people face to face. But the really shameful part is, that *people allow themselves* to be treated this way.

17

Years ago, when computers were new, I went to the home of an engineer who was working on the prototype of a verbally control and response computer.

My job, as a speech coach, was to help him use his speaking voice to "inter-act" vocally with the computer.

No big deal! Just talk - !

It turned out the engineer thought the computer was criticizing him, judging him and it implied the engineer was stupid!

It took me a moment to digest that condition. I could not come up with a link between computer vs human behavior.

The engineer was sweating, his shirt was soaked and he was actually trembling out of fear of the computer!

I managed to talk him down, have him understand the machine had no ability to judge human behavior, that he was in charge and doing a great job.

I was so glad to get out of there!

The internet is part of a machine! Turn it off!

The internet is an opportunity for deranged people to hide behind, stir up lies and trouble. People who are true and honest don't need to hide. Don't be a part of it; don't respond to any negativity, name calling, lies or "trash talk".

Don't let people control you, especially people you don't know!! People you can't see and can't pin down.

You're better than that – turn off the computer! Read a book, lift yourself up – do it for **YOU.** You're going to have a long and beautiful life - and that will happen as soon as you stop letting others influence you - use you.

BULLYING TODAY - BY MACHINES

On-line Bullying

It isn't enough for us to be bullied in the home, at school, on the sidewalk, at church and by your "friends," now we react to "machines" - "ibullying"! Little electronic machines, iphones, computers, smartphones - whatever phones - dominate our thinking, our perceptions, our life.

It continually astounds me how we let a little machine control our thinking, control our opinion of ourself. How we turn to a machine for help when under stress - a machine! We let a machine control our life - we are more of a robot than the machine is!

Unbelievable!

So where should we turn for advice? When we're lost, where do we turn? Can a living person help us?

WHERE NOT TO LOOK FOR HELP OR INFORMATION

Cyberspace...is an interactive domain of communication. It has no personality, no understanding of feelings, of judgment, of right or wrong. It's a "machine" that sends whatever information is put in it - "garbage in - garbage out".

The problem is, you don't know who is putting what information in it. It could be sincere, it could be lies, what - who is the source? Is the information a glitch in the works?

Is the information even, at all, valid…or is it just words intended to hurt someone, like machine gun fire, is the information randomly scattered, indiscriminately, like bullets to hurt anyone who accepts it? Anyone who steps in front of the flying bullets?

Twitter…is a means of listening to messages from a variety of sources. It was originally designed to advertise some event or product. At this time the messages have morphed into blather, opinions of people unqualified to speak on social issues. The information on Twitter is, essentially, useless, and people turn to it for "news" and guidance. Is this intelligent?

Facebook…is another means of social connection. It's a very down-to-earth means of "speaking" to friends and family, send current pictures and, in general, is a means of staying in touch with friends. It's difficult to be anonymous on Facebook.

As far as the influence on Twitter, Facebook, social media, use your self-control and inner strength, don't use it - it's a waste of your precious life.

Don't try to keep up with other people - stand by yourself, stand up for yourself.

Drugs…are a way to "drop out" of responsibility of life. It's a way to avoid having the boring, tedious task of getting through the day having to use intelligence, taking personal responsibility for one's life; it's a way to avoid having concern for others.

It is a total means of avoiding any work, any involvement in caring about, caring for, caring about the rights of others.

People on drugs want to be carried, looked after, attended to, cared about, thought about, talked about, suggested cures for, sweet helpful platitudes… it never ends.

THEY ARE BULLIES!!

It's all about them! Just like bullies, drug addicts seek love, attention, succorance. Their goal is to control you. And, yes, they do need help - professional help. Above all, don't pity them, that's feeding fire to fire.

SOME BULLIES SEEM TO BE POPULAR - DON'T BE FOOLED!

Without their "group," gang, backup support, some kind of outside support, many people are helpless, weak and have to hide what they do. If they're "alone", they have to do things under cover, back bite, lie about you, set you up, pull any support out from under you… It's so easy when people trust you - you can bully them around.

GROUPTHINK

Members of a group, gang, homies, sisters, clubs and fraternities are all expected to think the same things, enjoy the same things, have the same opinions – it's a group of people with one head, one mind. On the outside it looks like they are all good buddies, close friends, happy.

Don't be fooled. There are bullies inside the group. They are a group of scared, lonely people.

Often, in a group, one person will be bullied by the others – he'll do or say exactly as he's told otherwise the group will hurt him or throw him out and he'll be alone. The reason someone is in a group - gang- is because they are scared, weak-minded people who are afraid to be alone. Groupthink members are weak-willed, empty headed people easy to manipulate.

Surprisingly, there are bullies who bully bullies and the bullied bully is clueless! This situation is a form of Groupthink where the "victim-bully" is set-up to tease the target victim – you! They're encouraged to put on a show for the entertainment of the "super" bullies! Usually the "super" bullies stand back and watch the show; they are amused at how stupid one of their group is; he or she is being manipulated and is completely unaware!

Point out how the bully is being manipulated. When you're a part of a "show" like this, you're in the "arena", you can sidetrack the bully who is verbally attacking you by pointing out how the bully, he or she is being used. Point out the smirks on the faces behind him so he can readily see he is, also, a target. You might be doing him a favor. At least it distracts him from you.

ON THE SIDELINES. Surprisingly when there's a fight between a bully and a target, the onlookers often take the bully's side. Why? They assume the bully will win and want to be on the winning team. Onlookers have no loyalty to anyone; they're in groups because they're afraid to be alone. They're actually afraid of the bully themselves. They focus on you to keep the bully away from them.

Even though you may be the target, the bully has no friends – should she lose the battle, she loses her audience and their respect.

THE CHALLENGE – MORE GROUPTHINK

Everybody's doing it – are you going to chicken out?

Another example of Groupthink; you're pressured to do what everyone else does. If you don't, no one will like you, you'll have no friends, you'll be all alone. What's worse than being "alone" – no one to tell you what to do or think!

> Think on your own. Think about what's right and wrong to do.
>
> Just because someone says it's the right thing to do, deep down in your heart, do you really believe that? Are these people controlling you to make them feel powerful? Are you feeding their ego at the expense of yours?
>
> People who run in groups, "gangs" are the ones who are afraid to be alone. They need you to bolster their confidence. Avoid them; don't let them use you.
>
> Then, when you get in trouble, where are they? "Too bad," they say. "I wish I could do something, - I've got my own problems…" The result of groupthink is – you're left holding the bag! Now, you're really "alone"!
>
> Think for yourself.

COPING WITH GROUPTHINK

When the "gang" pressures you to do something – don't *be pushed around*. The "gang" doesn't care about you. If you don't do what they want, they lose their strength, their power - control over you. You think they're friends - you don't want to lose friends.

But, they are **not friends** – they are a scared, lonely group afraid of losing *you.*

Keep some phrases on hand, such as: "I'm not up to it tonight." "You go ahead; I'll go next time." "It's not something I enjoy." "I'd rather catch up on my… reading, homework, fix the car, see my brother…" and stick with that story. They'll counter saying:

"Why? You could do it later"… You'll get a lot of pressure, but take control over your own decisions.

> *Harry, a special needs person, was a man I worked with at a large company. He was slow at his work and easily upset. No one talked to him except me.*

I stood up for him, got the "tangled" ideas from his assignment removed or simplified so he had an easier time under-standing what he was to do.

> *I learned his father hated him and his mother was the usual, browbeaten housewife who never stood up for him. He had no friends but he was married to a woman like himself and they had a little dog they adored.*

> *A certain man at this place disliked me intensely and was ridiculing me. My "friend," Harry, someone I had helped, took this "bully's side with much pleasure. I was shocked, but said nothing.*

> *Later that day Harry realized what he had done. He walked around with his head down and we never spoke to each other again.*

> *He fully realized how he had shot himself in the foot. I still hurt for him, but I couldn't trust him after that.*

THE BOTTOM LINE…

DO YOU REALLY WANT CHANGE?

There is only one solution to bullying, only one person can stop it,

<u>YOU</u>

YOU have to get involved in your own rescue, in your own maturation, in your own inner strength. Bullying does not end - ever. It just changes form from place to place.

Think of bullies as your chance to learn about yourself, your weakness; this is your chance to mature into an independent, self-controlled person.

In a way, a bully is helping you to develop inner strength, inner growth - wisdom, your level of maturity, of development to a new level of growth you'd never have had otherwise. The bully is doing you a favor!

The bully's perspective

Why does someone hurt you - you've done nothing to them?

So, your first concern is, "What can I do to make *them* stop?"

The answer is,

> *"You **can't**." You can't change other people.*

But… when you **change yourself**, bullies and problems can be better managed.

Life is not always a pleasant place, but the majority of the time, we have the opportunity to lift ourselves out of the darkness into the light. Only you can do this, and it's scary, at first. You may feel alone, worried, not trust anyone. Don't get discouraged.

BULLIED FOR BEING GAY

This situation was put in its own category as Gays have suffered every insidious kind of bullying there is. I just read in the news another, gay 15 year old boy committed suicide.

In the Old Testament it says being gay is an abomination. That's the OLD Testament.

Then, if you notice, God sent his ONLY BEGOTTEN SON to teach us a more intelligent way to "judge" others. You DON'T!!

That's the _**NEW**_ TESTAMENT. People who judge others for their "differences" from the average person in any society are the SINNERS! The people who hate Gays, who speak out against them are _sinners_! Jesus said, "Love ye one another."

You can't have it both ways. You can't be a Christian and condemn any other person who is trying to live his or her life in a way different from yours.

For Christ's sake, treat them with courtesy and kindness. If they are "lost" people, all the more to treat them with kindness and Christian love.

STRATEGIES TO COPE WITH BULLIES

1. GET REVENGE ON THE BULLY– fight fire with fire!

This is one method to stop the bully – but does it work?

Call her trash names when you see her; wave your arms in the air and point your finger at her - show everyone how bad she is! Key the bully's car; hit the windshield with a baseball bat. Show the bully how clever you are.

Post trash about him on social media – it doesn't matter what you say – no one can prove anything!

Follow social media as much as possible - focus on it, find out what bullies are saying about you and come back at them twice as hard with stuff about them.

Send thoughts of hate, destruction. Thoughts are "things" – they have power; they can do some real damage!

There's just one problem with this method – when you spend your life-energy on "evil," the evil energy surrounds *you* and *drags you down*. Focusing on them eats away at your quality of life – *it's all about them!*

Your energy is focused on the bully – what's he doing? What's she thinking about? What'll he do next? The reality is the bully

27

has no idea these thoughts are coming her way; if she doesn't "accept" them, they have little power. When "evil" thoughts are not accepted, they have to go somewhere - so, they come "home" to you – they belong to you. But, they build up momentum on the way back!! "Evil" thoughts come "home" stronger than when they went out!

Don't wish evil on anyone! It *will come back* to you!

When your thoughts are focused on the bully, he has power over you – it's a form of control. You're doing exactly what the bully wants –you're feeding his ego - big time!

The Law of the Universe

But, the Law of the Universe *will* get your revenge for you – you don't have to do anything!

I promise you *there is* someone who watches over you and who sees all you do! It's *not* what others do that matters, *it is what you do* that matters! Deeds are balanced out when you least expect it - *what goes around, comes around.*

So, maybe revenge is not such a good idea after all!

2. "STARVE" THE BULLY

As far as possible, don't have eye contact.

Don't respond to email, Facebook or any media.

Do all you can to stay out of the way of the bully.

If you know his or her habits, hang outs, friends, stay away from them.

As difficult as it may be, keep as far away from the bully as you can.

If a friend of a bully should suddenly be nice to you, watch out! They're up to something. Say nothing to them except the weather is beautiful in Brazil.

They call you names.

People call you hurtful names, make fun of you, you decide just to ignore them – the names they call you are not true! Why listen to them? Names are meaningless words! How can "words" - hurt you?

You know the old nursery rhyme: "Sticks and stone may break my bones, but words will never hurt me."

So not true!! Words can cut far worse than any knife! Sharp, hurtful words can leave deep wounds that never heal. A physical wound heals and can be forgotten. But often, hate-filled words leave damage forever.

You hope by ignoring the name-calling, the bully will get tired of the game and move on; the bully will be bored and look for a more responsive target.

Hopefully, if you ignore them, they'll get tired of the name-calling and change tactics.

Turn off the social media.

One way to ignore the bully is to turn off the social media; forget there's a whole world of "important" people out there talking about you! Is there a world beyond cyberspace? Is there Life outside the 'net?

> **Actually, yes**! There is life outside the 'net - for *intelligent* people!

You can take control of your thoughts by ignoring the messages – shut off the bells and whistles that signal a text. You actually could **NOT RESPOND**! That would give you total control! But, can you turn off your mind? Can you stop giving them the attention of your thoughts – energy?

In the days of long ago, when there were knights of honor and damsels in distress, a nobleman, a knight's station, was far above that of the common man - the knight was important, the commoner was not. Therefore a knight would never stoop to argue with a commoner – it would be an insult for him to pay any attention to someone beneath his station! Commoners were too insignificant to get any attention.

This was a part of their training – they had to uphold tradition; be above ignorance.

Do the same – ignore the bully and build up your self-esteem. You're important – not the bully!

Again, this strategy might seem like a good idea, but, it too, has problems. It's possible instead of "ignoring" the problem you're just stuffing that negative energy deep down inside you.

3. ILLNESS - NEGATIVE PSYCHIC ENERGY:

Because you don't think consciously about something - you think you're ignoring it, that doesn't mean that it's not in your mind. It could be very much in your mind – 'way down deep inside. The negative energy could be pushed far down inside your psyche, stored in the body some place where it doesn't belong.

This stored negative energy may cause a physical reaction: Your body may speak to you through: hives, rashes, mononucleosis, cancer, migraines, ulcers or acne – your body is telling you to get rid of the unwanted substance – stop pretending to be ok, by ignoring the bullying.

It's not ok!

Admit to yourself that you're unhappy; keep the fear outside - don't let it fill up your insides and then boil over into some illness that destroys your physical or mental health. When you admit to pain, you accept it, then you can start the process to heal.

Don't say things like, "It'll go away. I'll forgive them and it will pass." "Rain falls on the just and the unjust alike." It's not a weakness to admit to weakness! It's a strength to seek help, to ask for help.

The trick is in knowing *who* to ask for help.

If you ignore these "messages" they could possibly get worse! The body's job is to keep *you* healthy, keep *you* operating in the best possible way; ignoring the negative energy of the bully may not be the best plan for you.

Maybe asking yourself why what the bully says and does hurts you. What is lacking within you, that you pay any attention to what the bully thinks or does? What, within you, maybe needs fixing?

> *A woman brought her 12 year old son to me for counseling. When she entered my home, she insisted I close all the drapes so her husband couldn't find her. If possible she wanted complete darkness. Not possible, it was early afternoon. Some light was evident.*
>
> *When I saw her son, even in the darkened room, I was stunned. His face was aflame with acne - aflame! He kept his eyes focused on the floor.*
>
> *My inner reaction was one of shame, horror and great sadness for this boy. His face was the expression of hate, anger, fear, repulsion and self-loathing. I almost cried for his sadness.*

31

The mother explained the father was rough on the boy, a ruthless expectation of high standards and perfection in general - extreme bullying.

She went on to say the father wanted the son to go to a military school and she asked me what should she do...send him to military school or keep him home?

Without hesitation. I said, "Send him to military school! Get him away from his father!"

They left. I don't know what her decision was. But, almost anyplace would be better than "home".

4. UNDERSTAND THE BULLY

All bullies are hungry for attention; they'll do anything to keep you focusing on them. Some bullies are not intelligent, they gain attention by physical force, no brain - all brawn. They're humiliated by their lack of academic skill and try to distract you from that. They use physical intimidation to control you.

A bully may be someone who is insecure and by treating others badly, that gives him power, identity, recognition. He's insecure, needs to hurt others to feel that he's strong - no one can hurt him if he can control you.

By laughing at you and pointing out your weaknesses, a bully may be distracting others from seeing her weakness. As long as she keeps the focus is on *you*, no one will see how weak *she* is.

My great grandson, Xavier, at age 12, was teased a lot because of how "pretty" he is - really- quite handsome. He finds it very tiresome for people to constantly comment on his looks.

One day, after hearing more derogatory comments about his looks from the same boys, he stood in front of them

32

and said, "It wasn't funny then and it's not funny now."
They left him alone after that.

Remember, the bully usually travels in groups, gangs. This is a sure sign of weakness; if he needs others to back him up, that means he can't do anything alone; he is scared of being alone; he might fail, but with a gang to back him up he feels strong enough to hurt you.

The bully needs attention. By focusing his negativity on you, and you respond, the bully has your attention, your "energy." Anytime you give something your energy, your thoughts, your focus, it's a type of "gift." In a sense, you are cooperating with the bully to control you.

5. DON'T COMPARE YOURSELF TO OTHERS

Each person is unique. Even identical twins have some aspect that is different from the other person. No two people are exactly alike, so why compare them? It's useless. Someone may be smarter than you, better at sports, bigger eyes, bigger feet – who cares?

For every single thing you may have in common with someone, there are dozens of ways you're different. Comparisons are a waste of time.

6. COMPLAIN TO "AUTHORITIES"

Many advisors tell you to report bullying to an authority, the principle of the school, your teacher, an officer, your parents or pastor.

Yes, you can start there and that's a good idea. Especially if there is physical harm - that should definitely be reported. **Physical harm is not acceptable**.

However, much of bullying is mental, quiet, subtle, sneaky – you can't put it into words. You say someone pushed you or made a face or laughed at you… this kind of bullying is hard to define, describe. You may end up looking like a whiner and the bully gets a good laugh.

Teachers, parents, friends and pastors may be far too busy to listen to your complaints when they can't easily be fixed. They will offer some well-meaning advice which is not at all helpful, things like:

>Move on, forget it - it's over.

>Just ignore it; it you don't give it attention, it'll go away.

>Think about something else.

>They don't really mean that; they just say those things, but they don't really mean them.

>Don't let it get to you.

>Are you sure? Maybe you don't understand – maybe you're mistaken – maybe you….

>Be nice to them and they'll be nice to you.

>Give them a chance, maybe they'll change.

>Maybe you misunderstood

>I went through that – you'll get over it

>You're too sensitive; you need to lighten up.

>Well, they're from a bad home…

They're disadvantaged (so, it's ok if they beat you up)

ALL THIS PUTS THE BLAME ON *YOU*! They suggest *you* need to adjust to negativity! Don't buy into it! Don't add guilt to your inner pain. Don't shove your pain deeper inside you.

7. THREAT OF PHYSICAL HARM

Your role in a physical battle is:

    1. Don't respond to any challenges.

    2. Don't go to where you think a battle may start.

    3. Get out of there **NOW**, any way you can. This is a lose/lose situation.

8. THE BIBLE IS A TWO-WAY STREET

It was a sunny, lazy afternoon. I was home from work, slightly under the weather; there was a knock at the door. Two lovely ladies were there suggesting something like they wanted to save my soul from damnation.

Here was an offer I couldn't refuse.

When we were seated in my living room they asked me to get my Bible. I asked, "Which edition?" I had 6 different interpretations to choose from. I prefer KJV. I also had the Quran, Book of Mormon, The Teachings of Madame Blavatsky, Conversations With God, The Bhagavad Gita... You never know who's going to come up to your front door...

They asked me to read several passages, all of which had to do with, "repent, you're doomed, you're a sinner, no hope for you!...you have to be cleansed from evil within you..., you're going to burn in Hell, you're born in sin, and more of the same.

In exchange for their edification, I asked them to read some passages: God is love, God created you out of love, God is all-forgiving, ask, and God will help you. Jesus. the Savior of Mankind came to lift us up, hope, Love, redemption, forgiveness...

Uhm, what about those passages...?

They left.

My point is, in the Bible are wonderful passages filled with uplifting guidance, hope, cheer, loving words of forgiveness, hope - all there if you want it.

      Or,

There are passages of doom, you're a dead duck from the get-go, born in sin, die in sin, burning forever in Hell - what's your preference?

Heaven or Hell?

If you want to feel loved, strong, a worthwhile human being, fill your mind with all the good thoughts possible. Feed you soul with happiness, choose Life. Single out the uplifting passages from the Bible, or your Book of choice and "think on these things".

COMMON BULLY TACTICS: HOW TO COUNTER THEM

I posed a general question to my class, "Who's a bully here?" One young man raised his hand and said, "I am." I asked, "Why do bullies do what they do?" He replied with a smile, "Because it's so easy."

Who makes it "easy"?

You do.

Let's explore some options for you on how to recognize some bully strategies, tactics, and how to counter them. There are many kinds of bullies; these are just a few of the most common ones.

STALKING

This is actually terrifying. I've been stalked at least 3 times. It is unnerving and terrifying. Where is he - her? You arrive home from anywhere. The phone rings when you step in the door. It's him-her for the tenth time, or more, that day.

They knock on the door, a surprise, unwanted visit. They smile at you - what are they doing wrong? They just want to be friends.

Your heart is pounding, you drop things, can't concentrate on anything you're doing. You're constantly thinking about the stalker - why is he/she doing this? Why? You might or might not even know the person.

You look at the window, they're standing across the street, smiling. Notes come in the mail, some are stuck on your car windshield...there's no escape.

My daughter just reminded me, some "stalkers" are really wanting to be friends - they like you, admire you. But, you have no interest in being their friend. How, in good conscience, can you get rid of someone who likes you, a puppy dog panting with love...?

Some people just don't take a hint, or even a forthright statement of your choices. Some people, you can look them direct in the eyes and state, "Leave me alone. I'm busy, I'm tired, we have nothing in common..." They don't get it. They cry, sob big, sloppy tears - nose, eyes, mouths dripping with disgusting fluids, "I'll kill myself!"

What to do?

Suggested solution

You can try for a restraining order - it's piece of paper with a lot of big words, won't save you from a bullet.

Above all - do not attempt to reason with them, explain your feelings, don't ask them "WHY...?" **Stop any interaction** - verbal or physical

DO NOT agree to them meet them for a "talk" alone, in the car of what *they* want... very dangerous thing to do!!

STAY AWAY FROM THEM! THEY ARE DANGEROUS - CRAZY!

I was lucky. I did nothing, and eventually they got tired of the game. However, I am still unnerved to this day by the sneaky, dark, phone calls, notes, staring eyes - they are sick people.

It's almost impossible to reason with a sick mind. Get professional help.

FACEBOOK

Why bother even talking about social media? If you're serious about stopping bullying, negative feelings, back-stabbing, then shut down the social media and fill your self with calm, happy thoughts.

Use your head. Why pet a snake just because you're lonely?

Suggested solution

If you really want a better life, more control over your own life, control over your feelings, thoughts, choices - get off social media.

Turn it off. Click it off. Unplug it.

Learn to read. Study the harpsichord.

MAKING FUN OF YOU

Teasing you, laughing at you, you have a big nose, too tall, too short, too smart, stupid…fuzzy hair, no hair, clumsy, slow thinker…fat, skinny - who ever you are, what ever you are - someone, somewhere will laugh at you.

I knew this girl in college who was 6' tall, 120 pounds, long skinny legs, long skinny arms, short, frizzy hair, long skinny feet and, she wore eyeglasses.

When she walked, she didn't walk, she "roller skated" down the hall with her arms swinging like propellers.

It was too much. Everyone (the girls) fell into hysterics! Over it all, her name was (something like) "Willie Dumdilly". It was all too much - hysterical laughter! I suspected she knew people laughed at her but she never let on. She always appeared calm.

We didn't see her at school for about 2 months or so, but when she came back, it appeared she had taken charge of her life.

Her hair was straighten and curved nicely around her features. She walked like everyone else and her arms were calm, but the best part was, she had changed her name to "Anna Johnson"!

She didn't whine, cry about the teasing, didn't lick her wounds - she took charge of her life and changed her outward appearance!

I was so proud of her.

Suggested Solution

It just shows you how determination and positive action can change your life and the opinion of everyone around you. Think about losing weight, gaining weight, wear better-fitting clothes, better hair style…

HIDING YOUR ITEMS

Years ago I worked at hp, the only "girl" among all engineers. The men took great delight in hiding my purse, hiding my chair and my tools.

Inside of me, I was furious! But that's exactly what they wanted. So I left my purse in the car under my "stuff". When they hid my chair, I simply stood at my place and worked, even though it was a sit-down position.

I learned to carry my lunch in my pocket so they couldn't hide my food. And, I borrowed the tools near me - the men never mentioned that. Eventually they got tired and stopped.

And!!! In spite of how they tried to make me miserable, some of them still tried to date me!! Are you serious! NO, never happened! Why reward bad behavior?

Suggested Solution

When people try to make you miserable, like hiding your tools, your lunch, your chair, your homework - you have to think ahead. When you can't stop the incessant, *boring*, teasing, come up with ingenious ways to take care of your needs. You may end up wearing a haz-mat suit to work - so be it.

HIT YOU

Physical abuse is an indication of desperation on the part of the bully. When he/she is lost for intelligent words or ideas - they'll resort to physical bullying. *Get help immediately!*

This is when, as you can, get legal help, the police, the Principal, your parents. It won't stop until you stop it. It'll get worse. If you don't put a stop to it, the other person will think it's ok with you.

As soon as you realize your friend is a physical abuser, leave! Just Leave! Don't listen to why he or she does that - bad childhood, confused life, needs love/understanding. Tell him or her to **go for help, you are not qualified.**

QUESTIONING YOU

This is an annoying, mind-twisting trick bullies use to keep you focusing attention on them. They batter you with questions: Where did you go? Why did you go there? *Where did you really go? (That one's my favorite - it assumes you're lying)* Who was there? Was so and so there? Are you sure? What time did you leave?…. you get the idea, it never ends.

Suggested Solution

If you enjoy being bullied, then sit there, upset, crying, try to explain, answer, respond, assure, beg, plead, promise anything… to prove you were just out for a walk and got an ice cream. The bully won't believe anything you say anyway.

You have two choices here:

1. Get tied in knots of nerves, sleepless nights of anguish, get headaches, rash, pimples…

or,

2. Walk away, shut the door behind you and don't look back.

42

SET YOU UP

At times people will set you up so you're stuck with a bill, get stiffed for a loan, drive the gang somewhere and they ditch you, you drive them somewhere, park the car, take the ticket and no one helps to pay for gas or parking.

Suggested Solution

For awhile I was friends with people, different groups. In one group, I was always expected to drive, pay gas and parking. Another group expected limousine service. Another group wanted someone to fill in an empty space at a dinner or program.

Do you see how I was asking for problems!!! When I finally figured out how I was being used, bullied, I just avoided them all after that. I was hurt, yes, but I didn't need "friends" like that. I never heard from any of them later.

BREAKING, STEALING, YOUR THINGS

Some people have nice things and other people don't. So, people steal nice things to balance the equation. When you confront them for taking, breaking, losing or forgetting to put back something of yours, it' a subtle method of bullying you. The bully is bringing you down to his/her level of "poverty" or lack of looking good.

It might be your new games, iPhone, CD's, DVD's - whatever. The bully promises he or she will return the thing, just as soon as they can. They don't. And, you never see it again - plan on it.

Suggested Solution

Don't mention the item again. Don't ever loan them anything again, for no reason, for no amount of time, never. No matter how much they ask, promise or get mad, don't loan them anything, again. If you do, then don't get mad because they lost it. They *will* lose it.

STAB YOU IN THE BACK

You are well-qualified for a promotion, an award, recognition of some type or an opportunity to gain an advancement you very much wanted. Maybe there are two or three of you being considered for the opportunity.

Suddenly, you're dropped out of the running and someone else got the award. What happened? You've probably been stabbed in the back, someone lied and he or she said you didn't want the award, that you lied to get considered for the prize - you didn't do the work at all...

> *For 15 years I was the principle singer in the church choir and the substitute director between professional directors.*
>
> *We hired a new director, a young man, well qualified who, he told us later, was dying of Aids. He still directed the choir as ill as he was, but there was no doubt he was working under great stress.*
>
> *Another woman in the choir, new to us, wanted to be the principle singer, so she lied to this physically weak and tired director, that I said very negative, hurtful things about him. That never happened.*
>
> *He called me in is office and said, "Get out! You're out of the choir!" I was stunned!*
>
> *Almost immediately this woman (a psychiatrist!) did all the solos! The lights went off in my head, and yes, I was angry - stabbed in the back, by a church member... how low can you sink?*

Suggested Solution

There's not a lot you can do. Once someone's mind has been poisoned against you, you lose. You might confront the offender in front of his or her friends of what they did, but you will probably end up looking like a jealous loser. The person who stabbed you in the back couldn't care less about how you feel.

IGNORED AT LUNCH – MAKE YOU SIT ALONE

You're at the cafeteria with your tray looking for a place to sit down. You choose a seat near the end of a long table. Other students hold their trays, look at you and the empty seats and walk by.

They walk to a table farther away and sit together. Once in awhile they will glance at you and maybe smile a little. They never talk to you.

They're locking you out - ignoring you.

It is so rude, hurtful.

Suggested solution

Try to keep a happy look on your face. If someone looks at you, look pleasant, not hurt or upset – if you can.

Look for someone else who might be sitting alone or with a small group. After lunch you might go up to them, ask if you might sit with them next lunch period. They might say, "Yes," or they might say, "No." But at least you tried.

If the "bully" group ever comes over and wants to be friendly, be careful, go with them if you want, but be careful – it may be a trick.

Don't trust anyone in the bully group until you've known them for a long time.

NAME CALLING

Maybe you're from another country, you have an accent. Maybe you're very tall or very short –not the average height. Maybe you're poor at sports, you have a physical problem where you can't run, catch anything or jump. Maybe you're overweight, have some color of skin or wear different clothes. Or maybe you have poor eyesight or hearing impaired.

All these things make you "different".

Suggested solution

Whatever name they call you try to see some humor in it, try not to let it bother you. Stay calm, don't react.

Above all – *don't cry*! If you cry, that just makes them happy.

If possible, with good humor, agree with what they call you and then point out some problem they have and laugh.

Once in high school, for no reason, this girl made fun of my nose. She said "Your nose looks like you walked into a wall." I looked at her nose and said, "You look like you caught your nose in a screen door."

Then she got mad at me! and I was surprised! Why would she get mad at me for doing to her exactly what she just did to me?

But, that's people for you. If you decide to do this –make fun of them, that's ok, but be careful. Today people get violent for no reason.

Hopefully, they'll get tired of their stupidity and leave you alone.

FOLLOW YOU HOME

Sometimes bullies will follow you home and make fun of you along the way. This can be dangerous and scary. If you have to walk long blocks or open spaces where they can tease you by running a bike at you, or running at you, knocking things out of your hands, knocking you down or treating you rough, you're in a difficult position.

Suggested solution

Today, thank goodness, we have cell phones. You can keep your phone on some emergency number if you need help. Don't let them take the phone away from you. Keep it on a chain on your body somewhere.

Or, you can talk to some of the neighbors along the way ahead of time. Ask them if that you have a problem with bullies, can you come into their house and stay until help comes or the bullies leave. You might have your parents talk to the neighbors and explain the problem.

Let the authorities, police, know of the problem and ask them to drive by when you're on your way home.

LAUGH AT YOU

Being laughed at can be hurtful, but only *if you allow it to hurt you*. Usually what people laugh about is really stupid. If you can dissect the words and ideas the bully is using, you'll find he or she makes no sense.

If you get upset, cry or get angry – the bully wins.

Suggested solution

When someone laughs at you for a stupid reason, look at them, sigh and say, "That's really stupid. Is that the best you can do?" Then, whatever they say next, listen, think and say, "That's not much better." And walk away.

If you think what they say is true, then smile and say, "Hey, Alex, that was pretty good – you're actually a lot smarter than you look." And walk away.

Or, ignore the whole thing. Walk away. Don't look back.

TEASE YOU

This kind of bullying can be very annoying. Nothing can be so irritating as someone teasing you over and over and over…

I had a friend in high school who had a 6 year old red-headed brother. He was so-o spoiled. His parents favored him - he got to do anything he wanted. One day Dolores and I were in the front room talking and David kept untying my shoe. I'd tie it, he'd untie it. I'd tie it and he'd untie it. I asked him to stop – he just laughed. Dolores threw a book at him and it hit his hand. He went screaming for his mother. She was a big, red-headed woman with a BIG voice. She bellered at me, telling me her son could do whatever he wanted. David later became a drug addict and spent years in and out of jail.

Suggested solution

In this case, I should have just left my shoe untied. Dolores and I stopped being friends. People who enjoy teasing others have a serious personality defect. It's a type of torture. As soon as you can, leave. You may also mention that this type of behavior is not normal and a professional evaluation might be helpful.

LEAVE YOU OUT OF THE TEAM

When a group or person has to choose who to be on a team, that person will choose his buddies or the best players. You may not be good at the game or the chooser just doesn't like you. You'd like to be a part of the team.

Suggested solution

Don't act disappointed. Wish the team well, tell them you know they'll do a great job and make their side look good. Take it on the chin. No one wants someone who is not a good loser. They may choose you next time - they probably will.

LEAVE YOU OUT OF PARTIES

The popular kids have parties and invite each other- you're never invited. When they tell you what a great time they had, smile and agree with them. They're hoping you'll feel bad; they may ask you if you'd like to go sometime. Don't be too quick to say "Yes" – it may be a trick. Say, "I'll let you know." – nothing else.

There's no Suggested Solution. This is so hurtful. Give yourself the time to get over the hurt and find something good to make you happy.

BAIT YOU

This is when someone knows your weak spots and teases you about them. This baiting can be based on false information. Maybe you're insecure about your girlfriend or boyfriend. So the baiter says, in public, "Hey, I saw (Gary or Alisha) with another guy last night – they're cheating on you! They're seeing someone behind your back!" Or they say, "Davila's been trash talking you! You should hear what she said about you!"

Often you have a special friend you spend time with, let's say you're Genna, Nikki's your best friend. At some point, you're alone, Nikki's not with you. Alicia comes up to you, confidentially, "Genna, I know Nikki's your best friend, but I heard her talking about you - you should hear what she said!"

Of course you're alarmed and curious. "What did she say?"

Alicia looks very concerned and says, "I can't tell you," and walks away.

Now, you're angry with Nikki because you believed Alicia – Alicia has succeeded in breaking the two of you up, which was her only goal – to make trouble for you. And, you believed her.

Suggested Solution

To counter these situations, get all of you together, you, Alicia and Nikki, ask what exactly was said, who said what. You may be surprised that much of the talk is based on lies. If all of you stand together, no one can deny what was said.

When you respond to baiting, you feed fuel into the situation and call more attention to it. Try to ignore it – it's hard, but try.

At a moment when you feel calm, go up to the bully, say, "John (Tiffany) when you yell out at me, when you make fun of me, call me names, it calls attention to you as well as it does me. You look like a fool - you act like a clown. You may embarrass me, but you also embarrass yourself.

When the people laugh at me, they're laughing at you. They know you're doing this for attention, you're a clown putting on an act. They don't really like you, they're using you to entertain themselves, they're not your friends. I feel sorry for you."

Then calmly walk away, say no more.

SCHADENFREUDE (shah den FROY duh)

This is a wonderful German word meaning " malicious joy," or "harm-joy". People who appear to be your friend are secretly making fun of you or tormenting you - but they do it with "sympathy". When you have a problem; they appear concerned but secretly wish you harm - they secretly do what they can to destroy your self-confidence. This is usually a female – one of your "best" friends..

For example if you take a test and pass it, she'll ask you, "Did you pass the exam yet?" You say, "Yes." They'll frown slightly seem surprised and, again, ask gently, "Oh... you passed?" Sort of confused, you'll repeat, "Yes."

Then they'll frown more, look puzzled, surprised you passed the test. You're confused - they have you wondering what's wrong, what did you miss. Your "friend," the schadenfreude, is quiet and appears slightly worried. She appears to care about you but doesn't want to tell you anything that will hurt you.

Or, if you wear an outfit that you look good and feel good in, the schadenfreude looks at you with a slight frown and say, "Did you get that on sale?" You say, "No, it's custom made." She'll frown, pause and say, "I see…" leaving you to wonder what's wrong.

Suggested Solution

When you suspect your "friend" is silently critiquing you, it's pointless to stay friends with her. The more you relate to her, she gets stronger, you get weaker. Be polite, but keep your physical and emotional distance.

When she's surprised that you got the promotion, (passed the exam, got the job, look great in a new outfit or hair style), look directly into her eyes and smile sweetly. Say, "Jeanine, I notice whenever I achieve a goal, you seem surprised. Why is that?"

She'll be caught off guard, maybe say something like, "What do you mean?" She's stalling, caught off-guard – she knows full well what you mean.

Keep smiling; look directly into her eyes, say sweetly, "You haven't noticed? When I do well at something you seem surprised? Why is that?"

By now, she's on to you. She's annoyed at having been caught at her own game. But she'll parry. She'll say, "Christine, I have no idea what you mean. I care about you, and want you to do well." She'll stall for time to try another strategy.

You have won the battle – but not the war. Drop the conversation for the time, but be on guard. When she does it again, smile and sweetly say, "I appreciate your concern Jeanine." And drop it. She'll reconnoiter for another day. She'll keep trying – she hates to lose.

QUESTIONING YOU

Some people continually question you about what you did and why. They pin you down, ask question after question even when you have answered several times. They frown, look deep into your eyes, probe for the "truth". They seem genuinely interested, but actually are thinking of their next tactic to control you.

They ask: "Are you sure? What do you mean? How did that happen? Why did you (he, she they) do that? I don't understand, explain that to me. But why did you, he, she they do that? Are you sure? What do you mean?..." It *never* stops; the questions are *never* answered even though you have told all you can. The Questioner is toying with you – it's a game.

Questions are a way of controlling you, keeping your energy focused on them – your full attention is on them. The more questions you answer, the more energy you feed them, the more they control you - bull you.

Suggested Solution

The best way to handle "questioners" is to question them back; *take charge* of the interaction; take away their "power." Ignore their question, say, "I don't understand; what do you mean?" "Why do you ask that?" "Why do you need to know?" "What, specifically, is not clear?" This will keep them off-track until they can figure out where to go next. They may actually get tired of their own game! "Play" with them - people hate it when they lose at their own game!

Always smile sweetly when you talk to a Questioner. Look as though you're very interested in what they have to say.

USING SICKNESS TO BULLY

When someone is ill, you're expected to treat him or her with kindness and do what you can to make her comfortable. And yes, you should – we all should. Someone can't help being sick or handicapped – they need help and it's the right thing to do.

However, sometimes illness is used to bully people; the sick person wants to control you – he has found a way to get attention. If you leave, he'll have an attack of some kind. If you stay he'll fuss continually about his suffering. He may be a martyr, pretend to care about your discomfort by staying with him – you're trapped - if you leave, you're wrong; if you stay, you're wrong. Illness can be a way to toy with you, keep you under total control – you're miserable – you're bullied! They're happy.

CARMINE

*It was the first day of the new Semester. It was early, I was alone in the classroom waiting for the students, when an older student walked in. Her first words to me were, **"I'm going to die!"** Startled, I looked at her and saw long, white plastic tubes about 24" long and 1" in diameter hanging from her shoulders under her tiny blouse sleeves down to her wrists. I murmured some words of condolence. More students came in. Carmine walked up to each one and announced, **"I am going to die!"***

Before the whole class Carmine gave a lengthy explanation; she had pancreatic cancer and didn't have long to live. She had a 10 year old son who would be left alone – on and on. The tubes were for dialysis which she had at least once a week – she said.

It went downhill from there. Carmine took over the class, interrupted my lectures, stood up in class, pointed at me and laughed. It got to the point where I had to get the campus police to remove her from the classroom. It took weeks of bullying before I managed that.

Carmine got what she wanted –everyone focused on her! Her "illness" was a sham, a ruse to siphon someone's energy - and she did it well!

Suggested Solution

One way to handle people who bully you by "illness" is to be pleasant, but distant. When they complain avoid eye contact, reply, "I see…" or "Hmmm…"- nothing more. Don't engage them in conversation if possible. All they want is your attention, time and energy.

Or, if you're fed up with control tactics, you can seem concerned about their condition, say, "Oh, yes, Hermione! I've noticed how sickly you look - haggard, drawn, pale - actually kind of life less! I feel so sorry for you." Seem genuinely concerned. Hermione will be annoyed – she's used to someone comforting her. If you agree with her at how ill she is, she may stop her complaints for awhile – you hope! But – she'll be silently angry!

Or, do the reverse. When someone tells you how ill they feel or look, smile brightly and say, "Why Filipa! You'd never know! You look great! Your eyes are bright, your tongue is furry and you look so cheerful! Good for you!" Then walk away.

But, usually this is a way of life for hypochondriacs. For your sake, try to keep your mind on the pleasant events around you; keep yourself happy.

THE "VENTRILOQUIST" ANSWERS FOR YOU - won't let you talk

Someone asks you, "How do you like your eggs fixed?" Lila pipes up and says, "Jackie likes her eggs over easy." Or, "What's your opinion on global warming?" Lila butts in, "He has no opinion –none of that data is conclusive."

What to do? Usually Lila just goes right on talking totally ignoring you. Or, if you say, "I would like my eggs raw, please," Lila jumps in, "You never said that before, you must be kidding, raw eggs have pesticides…"

Suggested Solution

Lila, look at the other person and state, "I want 3 eggs and I want them *raw*. Thank you." Say it firmly, strong eye contact and don't change your voice in any way. *Ignore Lila,* don't smile. Lila means well, but perhaps she wants to *be you*; she may be jealous of your talents or popularity. If Lila comments on your choice, smile and sweetly and say, "I know what I want; but thanks for your concern Lila." And drop it until next time.

PHYSICAL FORCE

Under **NO** circumstances let anyone hit you, shove you, push you or pull you around. The other person will say, "Hey, I was only joking - lighten up!" It may look like the other person is joking or teasing, but *it's not*. Physical force is a way to control you, scare you, threaten you and bully you.

If you try to leave, or stop the "teasing," you'll look like you're no fun, like you're the problem – not the person teasing you. Don't worry about what other people think. *Don't allow yourself to be physically or mentally pushed around.*

> *I had two different women friends who, when I wanted to do something, and they didn't, would grab my sleeve and pull me away to their direction. They would just hold on to the sleeve as though it were a leash and pull me. It was infuriating. I'd order them to "STOP!" but they'd laugh.*

To this very day when I think of them I get angry with myself for allowing them to treat me that way. I should have, firmly and slowly, stated that I hated to be pulled and, don't do it again!

Suggested solution

As soon as you can, *leave the situation* – don't think it "will change," "they'll stop," - **IT WON'T STOP!** Do all you can *to avoid those people.* If you fight back, the bully will say, "Well you did it too!" – and he's right!

You'll look aggressive - the bully can hit back harder than before – now he's got a good excuse to show you who's boss! Don't react with aggression! *Leave, never go back! Don't accept an apology* or think "anyone can make a mistake' – wrong! Bullies control you by looking for forgiveness, pity. They'll cry, sob, apologize, buy you gifts - d***on't fall in that trap** – leave! Stay away from him or her.*

WHEN YOU FEEL ALONE LOST, LONELY, NO ONE CARES

When you're lonely, you're vulnerable, easy prey to someone who knows you'll do whatever he wants so you can have a friend. But, *people like this are not friends* – stay away from them. It's hard, but if you attach yourself to someone just because you want a friend so bad, you may be very sorry later.

Above all, stay away from people who want you to "try this", some drug, an unknown substance that will "make you feel good." Do not allow anyone to give you something to eat or smoke or use some substance that is not what your parents would want. Do not let anyone talk you into doing something you know is wrong or stupid – you will pay the price – not them. They'll sell you down the river first chance they get. These people are *not your friends.*

Take your time about trusting someone. Find friends of quality, join trusted organizations. Keep your standards for friendship high in trust and honesty.

This is definitely possible. It will take strength and patience on your part to find the right strategy for you to use.

But there are situations you can't avoid.

> *My stepfather made my life Hell. I was a kid, nowhere to go. I slept with my eyes open, got out of the house every day as soon as the sun came up. I finally got married to*

get out of the house. The worst decision I ever made. Do not think marriage is an escape. Get an education, a good job and get out of "home" as soon as you can.

WATCH AND SEE WHO IS NOT A BULLY

Keep your eyes open for people who stay out of the general crowd. There are people who keep a low profile to stay away from bullies. When you see someone who looks like a good person, talk to them, tell them you'd like to get to know them better. Maybe share a treat at lunch.

WHAT YOUR FRIENDS AND FAMILY SHOULD NOT DO.

Your friends and family care about you, they know how good you are. But, sometimes they give you advice that doesn't help you. They're not qualified to understand how much you hurt inside. Talk to a psychologist for a better understanding of your needs and perceptions of yourself and your relationships with others.

WHO TO ASK FOR HELP

This is the million dollar question....WHO to ask for help. Most people are reluctant, unprepared, inadequate to help you. They don't understand the depth of you pain. They lack confidence to talk to you, don't see a problem, would rather you didn't bother them...

CLERGY: If you talk to a clergy (priests, pastors, deacons, elders, counselors...) they'll give you the same guidance you're avoiding.

Clergy in general have a standard line to respond to emotional pain: Trust in God, turn it over to Jesus, pray about it, try to understand the other person - how they're hurting too... It's not as bad as you think.

Not a lot of real help, as I see it.

Usually Clergy have a line to sell; they're in the business of making money and keeping the line of patter alive in the congregation. I have found that there are a great many bullies alive and well in religious organizations. They use the church as a hammer to bully you to make you stay in line - put a guilt trip on you - it's confusing - these are "Christians"?

PSYCHIATRISTS: My experience with psychiatrists is - they're nuts. There may be one or two who have their feet on the ground, but you'd be lucky to find one.

PSYCHOLOGISTS: I've met some good ones, but stand back, be very careful. When people fiddle with your minds, it can be dangerous. Think ahead and listen carefully to everything they say and evaluate it carefully.

> At one time I was having recurring nightmares where I was escaping from "someone." In the dream I was terrified. The psychologist told me, to get a baseball bat and hide behind a wall. When my tormenter comes by, hit him over the head with the bat and I'd be ok.
>
> …? …What? This is advice - from a professional? Hit…someone, on the head?
>
> *Another psychologist I went to, as I told my sad tale, repeated over and over, "Oh, you poor thing," as she pushed a box of tissues at me. I was annoyed. I am neither "poor", nor a "thing". She said I was hostile. Well, what can you expect from a "poor thing"?*

That was the extent of my "help". Whatever it was, I got over it.

AN OLD LADY: Sometimes sitting down with an old lady and chatting about Life can be an enormous help. Most Old Ladies have graduated from the School of Hard Knocks and have much wisdom to share. They can see backwards and forwards and don't have an ulterior motive. They just love to talk.

Listen closely, Little One, learn.

Visit with one. Bring a tea bag and some cookies and prepare to have a most enjoyable time. You may be surprised at how much you'll learn, have fun and relax!

CLOSE FRIENDS: Talking to close friends is very risky - usually. There are so many pitfalls confiding in friends. Some of them delight in your weakness. Some of them take this opportunity to put you down further, "You should have…, well, why didn't you…, I told you before…" This doesn't help at all.

> *A woman was having trouble with her husband; he was bulling her. A friend advised her to divorce him. The woman did. The friend grabbed the man and married him herself.*

FINALLY, WHAT TO DO FOR <u>YOU</u>

You can either help yourself - or keep running in circles.

Take your mind off the bully – or die of a heart attack

Take your power for **you. Keep it.**

Every time the bully comes to mind:

1. Think of something else - immediately.

2. Volunteer at the local hospital, animal shelter, food bank. Take Karate

3. Meditate

4. Read poetry

5. Listen to classical music - Borodin, Faure, Tchaikovsky, Gershwin…

6. Avoid negative friends

7. Take Karate

8. Take classes in Communication, especially NON VERBAL Communication.

By watching people carefully, you can better understand how they think - anticipate what they'll do.

CAN WE SUE THE BULLIES?

Yes. And the result is, you'll probably lose. You'll be out money, time and energy and the bully will be the same – or stronger! Your chances of winning a bullying lawsuit are extremely poor. Of course it's possible, but you need fool-proof documentation and a strong constitution to stand up for yourself under incredible pressure.

If possible watch the Brett Kavanaugh - Dr. Christine Ford debate when Kavanaugh was up for Supreme Court Judge in 2018. Dr. Ford was under intense pressure to prove Kavanaugh attempted to rape her while they were at a high school house party. But, at the zero hour, Brett saved himself by bringing in a calendar from his high school days where he had everyday's events recorded on that specific day - an extremely organized journal written in each day's little square.

He "proved" that his events of the day in question did not allow a time and place to attempt to rape Dr. Ford.

Apparently I was the only person in America to find it extraordinary that a teen-age boy recorded his daily activity on a calendar, year after year - and, kept the calendar! I have never seen such meticulous notation before or since. The predominantly male jury found him blameless.

THE BOTTOM LINE

Don't trust **anyone**! If you have a secret - KEEP IT! Don't tell ANYONE your secrets! One day, they WILL BETRAY YOU.

Right now you're close to your very best friend, your best buddy, life-long friends…but, one day they WILL betray you! They WILL sell you out, make no mistake! Take care of yourself, trust only yourself.

I speak from painful experience - not once, not twice, but many times! How stupid can you get? You want to think well of your friends and hold them in high esteem - and you can do that. But never drop your guard. Things change, people change, circumstances change.

Always remember, "This friendship could change in a flash."

> *I had a certain friend who was just like me - I thought. We had everything in common, she helped me when I desperately needed help. I did all I could to support her in times of need. We were inseparable for many years.*
>
> *Then she married a man who was great - I thought. He was an investor and sold stock.. He wanted to invest my money with him and I had many misgivings. But, he was my best friend's husband - what could go wrong?*
>
> *I invested, he had lied, I sued, and won. My "best friend" came to my house, husband in tow, and she was carrying a large box of various things.*
>
> *The "things were gifts I had given her over the years. She took each thing out of the box and threw it at me, meanwhile yelling about how I treated her husband!*
>
> *He stood beside her with his head hanging in sorrow as though I had wronged him!*
>
> *I was stunned.*
>
> *Later, years later, he died and she wanted to be friends again. No. I was always polite and cordial, but we'll never be "friends" again. So sad.*

On the other hand, **DON'T YOU EVER** betray someone, lie about them, cheat on them, use them, ridicule them…always play straight, honest, keep your hands clean. Keep your self above board, be proud in yourself.

The only person's opinion of you that matters, *is your own*!

<u>Do not, ever:</u>

loan money to friends

loan your car

co-sign for anything

loan out your husband or wife for anything

hide, procure or buy any illegal substances for anyone

If you do choose to help a friend in any of these ways, expect it to blow up in your face. Plan ahead.

It will blow up.

Above all, have quiet time each day, alone, silent, breathe peace and freedom.

FORGIVENESS

In the Bible it tells us to forgive, no matter what, forgive - seventy times seven....

Easier said than done.

Sometimes you'd like to forgive. If you could, it would get a great load off your shoulders. Carrying anger, hate and emotional pain is very destructive to the body and mind - and tiresome. It never leaves you.

Sometimes someone has hurt you so bad, the thoughts, the pain, will not go away. You may use words like, "I forgive her, him, them - " but all the memories keep coming back, over and over.

Now you're in big trouble because you can't forgive and you feel guilty because you can't. You know you should, but you can't.

Now, not only are you suffering from emotional pain - and maybe fear, you're suffering from guilt because you can't forgive someone who caused you the emotional pain, suffering. But you're told you should.

What to do?

Is there any way out of this trap?

Yes. Admit it.

Go to your Source, the one you pray to and just tell it all, just be honest, candid, angry, puzzled, cry, scream, say how you hurt, how wrong it is… - whatever you feel, talk about it to the One. Use no substitutes, substitutes judge you, the One will not. In prayer, there are no "should's"; no, "You're just not trying hard enough's…". No chiding, no condemnation…

Just do the best you can.

> *I knew a sweet, little old lady. One of the kindest, gentlest people possible. Her mother died when she was 11, the father remarried and the stepmother hated the girl.*

> *The step mother had 5 girls and one boy. Her girls got new clothes, parties, all the fun of childhood. My friend got what her girls didn't want. She never got new clothes.*

> *She was bitter, angry and talked about her childhood often. She hated her stepmother. "But," she'd say. "I've forgiven her."*

> *Very often she'd tell the story of her childhood, her anger. "But," she'd say, "I've forgiven her."*

> *Hmmmm…had she?*

WHEN ALL ELSE FAILS...

Pray.

Yes, pray. But not pre-subscribed, memorized prayers, necessarily.

What's on your mind? What's hurting you? Or, why are you so happy lately?

You can pray when you're happy, you know. Every one likes to be thanked for a good dinner, a good day, not so hurting in the arthritis lately.

It doesn't matter what name you give when you pray, he or she will know who you mean. They're always listening, always awake, always waiting for a "Hello! I really need your help with this problem..." or you could say, "Oh, I had such a great day! Thanks for the sunshine and my green beans are coming up great!"

Everyone likes good news. And, in prayer bad news is very welcome.

Just tell it like it is, be honest about what you see, feel, understand. No excuses or reasons are needed - just talk, pretend this is someone who knows you well and you can trust.

You can even yell if you're really hurting - it's ok. You will not be judged.

BUT... after all I have said in this book about not trusting people, being betrayed, lied to, used... yes, it is a definite possibility, but...there are so-o many good people.

Given half a chance in Life, people will help where they can, when they can. In general, people are wonderful, caring, warm and sincere.

If you can approach life from this direction, you can feel secure, people in general are good.

Just don't get over-confident, don't have too high expectations. Keep your eyes somewhat open.

CONCLUSION

Don't feed the bully your energy. It's impossible to cover all the ways people bully. Don't accept negativity. Some people will like you and some won't – either way there's nothing much you can do about it. Be glad if someone likes you; if they don't like you, who cares!!

Focus on the good things in life. Find friends of good quality; fill your mind with positive thoughts. You have the power to make your life a good one. If you focus on what's good, the Law of the Universe dictates only good can come to you. It may take awhile, but *this is true.*

The poem, Desiderata - meaning, "what you should desire in Life" - has helped many people for many years. If you read it thoughtfully every day, it's one way to keep your mind in a good place, a healthy place, where you can heal and grow in inner strength.

DESIDERATA Words for Life

Go placidly amid the noise and haste,
and remember what peace there may be in silence.
As far as possible without surrender
be on good terms with all persons.
Speak your truth quietly and clearly;
and listen to others,
even the dull and the ignorant;
they too have their story.

Avoid loud and aggressive persons,
they are vexations to the spirit.
If you compare yourself with others,
you may become vain and bitter;
for always there will be greater and lesser persons than yourself.
Enjoy your achievements as well as your plans.

Keep interested in your own career, however humble;
it is a real possession in the changing fortunes of time.
Exercise caution in your business affairs;
for the world is full of trickery.
But let this not blind you to what virtue there is;
many persons strive for high ideals;
and everywhere life is full of heroism.

Be yourself.
Especially, do not feign affection.
Neither be cynical about love;
for in the face of all aridity and disenchantment
it is as perennial as the grass.

Take kindly the counsel of the years,
gracefully surrendering the things of youth.
Nurture strength of spirit to shield you in sudden misfortune.
But do not distress yourself with dark imaginings.
Many fears are born of fatigue and loneliness.
Beyond a wholesome discipline,
be gentle with yourself.

You are a child of the universe,
no less than the trees and the stars;
you have a right to be here.
And whether or not it is clear to you,
no doubt the universe is unfolding as it should.

Therefore be at peace with God,
whatever you conceive Him to be,
and whatever your labors and aspirations,
in the noisy confusion of life keep peace with your soul.

With all its sham, drudgery, and broken dreams,
it is still a beautiful world.
Be cheerful.
Strive to be happy.

Max Ehrmann (1927)

ABOUT THE AUTHOR

Carolyn Franklin

M. A. Communication Studies

M. A. Education

B. A. Psychology

30 years voice training (San Francisco Opera)

Voice/Speech improvement Coach

voicedynamicscf@yahoo.com

OTHER BOOKS BY CAROLYN FRANKLIN

Police Brutality: A solution

Adam: First man, or, first mouse?

Emotional Intelligence: Like yourself

Coping With Bullies: A gentle approach

You Can Catch More Flies With Honey: The Art Of Rhetoric, Persuasion, Manipulation, and Blarney

Your Voice – Your Personality The Total You

Women Bullying Women: An effect of Women's Lib

Rx For Your Communication Ills - The ULTIMATE Book on Communication

Women At Work: Win-Win Communication Strategies

#MeToo, NOW, Women's Lib, Just Say No: Why they won't work

Athena: Goddess of Communication Strategies

Welfare + Diversity: Social Suicide

The Story of Mary: Mayhem, mirth and miracles

How To Talk To A Texan And Other Foreigners: Understanding Everyone - We're Not All The Same!

The Princess And The Pee: Caring For A "Special Needs" Person

Just Be Your Self - Whoever That Is

Printed in Great Britain
by Amazon

36496323R00046